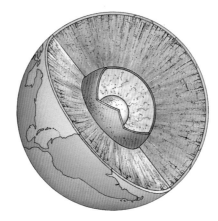

Around The World

CONTENTS

CREATIVE EDUCATION

Wow!

Incredible!

Our planet is a pretty amazing place. Here is just a small selection of record-breakers from nature and the world of human achievement.

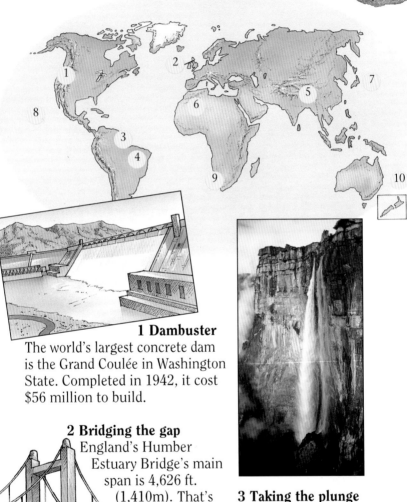

1 Dambuster

The world's largest concrete dam is the Grand Coulée in Washington State. Completed in 1942, it cost $56 million to build.

2 Bridging the gap

England's Humber Estuary Bridge's main span is 4,626 ft. (1,410m). That's the longest single span in the world.

3 Taking the plunge

At 3,212 ft. (979m), the Angel Falls, on the Carrao River in Venezuela, is the highest waterfall on earth.

4 River power

The Amazon is the world's mightiest river. It has a flow rate of 4.2 million cubic feet (120,000 cubic m) of water a second, which is the same as 6,000 baths a second!

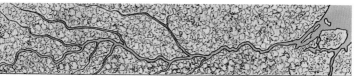

5 On top of the world

Mount Everest towers 29,029 ft. (8,848m) above Nepal, making it the highest peak on Earth.

6 Jumbo desert

The Sahara is the biggest desert in the world. It is about the same size as the U.S.

7 Metropolis

Tokyo-Yokohama's population is 27,245,000, making it the world's largest city.

8 Mighty sea

The Pacific Ocean is so huge, it covers nearly one-third of the planet.

9 Deep down

They don't go any deeper than the Western Deep gold mine in South Africa.

How deep?

It plunges to an incredible 2.4 miles (3.8km) below ground level.

10 Super spout

In 1903 the Waimangu geyser in New Zealand spewed boiling water to a record-breaking height of 1,500 ft. (457m).

The World Beneath Our Feet

In 1970 the Russians started drilling into the earth's crust, and by 1995 they reached their target depth of 9 miles (14.4km). It's the deepest hole in the world, but it is only 0.24 percent of the distance to the center of the Earth!

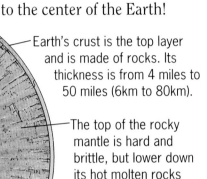

Earth's crust is the top layer and is made of rocks. Its thickness is from 4 miles to 50 miles (6km to 80km).

The top of the rocky mantle is hard and brittle, but lower down its hot molten rocks flow like molasses.

The core is mostly nickel and iron and is very hot, probably a scorching 8,100°F (4,500°C).

Cracking crust

Earth's crust is not just one big sheet of rock. It is cracked and broken into huge pieces that move about. Where two pieces of crust crash into each other, they push up mountains and create volcanoes.

Rocks

There are three main groups of rock on earth.

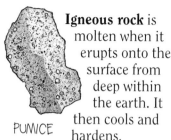

Igneous rock is molten when it erupts onto the surface from deep within the earth. It then cools and hardens.

PUMICE

Sedimentary rock is made up of layers of bits of rock and the remains of plants and animals that lived millions of years ago.

SANDSTONE

MARBLE

Metamorphic rock forms when rocks are changed below ground by great heat and pressure deep within the earth.

Turned to stone

Many sedimentary rocks contain fossils. Fossils are the remains of dead animals and plants that, over very long periods of time, have turned to stone.

Earth's vital statistics

Age: 4.5 billion years old.
Waist: 24,900 miles (40,000km) at the equator.
Weight: 6 sextillion tons.
Speed: orbits the Sun at 66,636 mph (107,208kmh).

Phew!

Hard and soft

The minerals found in rocks are graded according to their hardness. The softest mineral is talc, which is used as talcum powder. The hardest mineral is diamond.

TRILOBITE FOSSIL

AMMONITE FOSSIL

FOSSILIZED MAMMOTH'S TOOTH

5

Weather Watch

Earth is wrapped in a blanket of gases called the atmosphere. All our weather happens in the lowest part of the atmosphere, which contains a lot of water vapor. Water vapor is the gas form of water. Without it, we'd have no clouds, rain, hail, or snow.

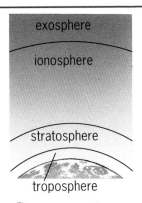

exosphere

ionosphere

stratosphere

troposphere

Clouds

When air rises up into the sky, it cools. The water vapor it contains turns into tiny water droplets. Millions of them join together to form a cloud. If the water droplets get too heavy for the air to support them, they fall as rain.

Rain-go-round

Rain is part of a never-ending water cycle.
1. The Sun's heat turns water into water vapor which rises up into the air.
2. As that water vapor, rises, it cools, and forms clouds.
3. In time rain falls from the clouds into rivers and streams, which run back to the sea. And so the cycle begins again.

Thunder and lightning

Thunderclouds are a mass of fast-moving air, water, and ice. When the water droplets and ice crystals crash into each other, they create an electrical charge that shoots out of the cloud as lightning. Thunder is the sound of air being heated up.

Disaster man

Don't be fooled by the saying "lightning never strikes twice." Between 1942 and 1977 Roy C. Sullivan was struck by lightning seven times.

And now for the forecast

In the days before orbiting weather satellites, people turned to somewhat less reliable forecasting methods. Pine cones were a favorite and were supposed to close up if rain was on its way.

All change

The fastest temperature change on record happened in South Dakota on January 23, 1943. At 7:30 a.m. it was –4°F (–20°C). Then at 7:32 a.m., it was 45°F (7°C) and fairly mild!

Come rain or shine?

Did you know that even supermarkets need to know what the weather is going to do? So if you ever see shelves and shelves of lettuce still sitting there at the end of a very wet day, it means that the forecast said it would be hot and sunny!

From Pole to Pole

If you traveled the world from top to bottom, you would come across many different regions, each with its own climate. It is hottest at the equator, where the Sun's rays hit the earth straight on. At the poles, the Sun's rays always strike at a slant, so their heat feels weaker.

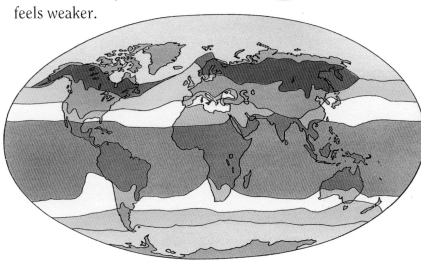

Polar/Tundra climate

Cold climate

Temperate climate

Subtropical climate

Tropical climate

Phew!
The hottest place on earth is Dallol, Ethiopia, where the average temperature is a scorching 93°F (34°C).

Brrr!
Parts of Antarctica have an average temperature of −72°F, (−58°C) making them the coldest parts of the globe.

Splash!
In Mawsynram, India, they get a record-breaking 467 in. (1,186cm) of rain every year.

Gasp!
Chile's Atacama Desert is the earth's driest place. Its annual rainfall is .004 in. (.1mm).

Polar/Tundra climate
Very cold all or part of the time. Only low-growing plants survive in places.

Cold climate
Short summers and long, cold winters. Most of the land is covered with forests of pine trees and other conifers.

Temperate climate
Western coastal areas have mild weather and regular rainfall. Inland and east coast areas are colder in winter, but warmer in summer. Lots of different kinds of plants grow in temperate climates.

Subtropical climate
Hot summers and mild winters. Mediterranean areas have hot, dry summers and warm, wet winters. Hot deserts can have no rain for years.

Tropical climate
Hot all year. In wet areas, there are huge rain forests. In drier areas, there are tropical grasslands.

Seas and Oceans

When the first man on the moon looked back at Earth it looked mostly blue. Why? Because less than a third of the planet is covered by land. The rest is ocean. The biggest ocean is the Pacific, which stretches between the east coast of Asia and the west coast of America.

EARTH FROM SPACE

Saltiest sea

Seawater is always salty. Warm seas are saltier than cold seas. The saltiest sea is the Dead Sea. Seawater is more buoyant than freshwater. The Dead Sea is so salty, it is impossible to drown in!

Danger below

Many ships have crashed into icebergs because they see only what is above the surface. Most of the ice in an iceberg is under water.

What a whopper

The cold seas around the Arctic and Antarctic are dotted with floating icebergs. The largest iceberg ever, seen off the coast of Antarctica, measured 12,000 square miles (31,200 sq. km). That's an area larger than Belgium!

Disaster strikes

In 1912 the luxury liner, the *Titanic,* hit an iceberg and sank, with the loss of 1,500 lives.

Down, down, down . . .

Small fry
Saltwater fish come in all shapes and sizes. The world's smallest fish is the 0.35 in. (8.8mm) dwarf goby, which lives in the Indian Ocean.

Colorful coral
Coral is found in the shallow waters of warm, tropical seas. It is made up of the skeletons of tiny animals called polyps.

Going down
Most sea animals live near the sunlit surface where there is plenty of food. Some, however, do survive in the blue-black depths below.

Giant squid
These huge sea creatures can be up to 60 ft. (18m) long. They boast the biggest eyes in the animal kingdom.

Headlights
Many deep-sea fish have lights on their bodies. They use these lights to attract their prey.

Deep drop
The deepest ever dive was by the bathyscaphe *Trieste* in 1960. With two men on board, it descended to 35,813 ft. (10,744m) into the world's deepest water, the Mariana Trench.

11

River Deep ...

Some rivers start as mountain springs. Others are fed by melting glaciers, and many are begun by rain and snow.

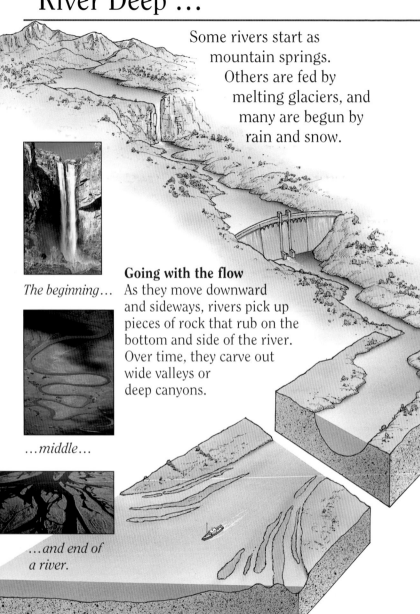

The beginning...

...middle...

...and end of a river.

Going with the flow

As they move downward and sideways, rivers pick up pieces of rock that rub on the bottom and side of the river. Over time, they carve out wide valleys or deep canyons.

ℒ*ongest rivers*

The two longest rivers are the Nile in Africa and the Amazon in South America. Both are more than 4,000 miles (6,400m) long.

and Mountain High

Top summits

	Everest 29,029 ft. (8,848m)
Aconcagua 22,834 ft. (6,959m)	
McKinley 20,320 ft. (6,193m)	
Kilimanjaro 19,340 ft. (5,894m)	
Mont Blanc 15,771 ft. (4,807m)	
Ben Nevis 4,432 ft. (1,350m)	

UK   EUROPE   AFRICA N. AMERICA S. AMERICA ASIA

Underwater mountains

The greatest mountain ranges on earth lie deep beneath the oceans. Some of their peaks break the water's surface as islands.

Underwater valleys

Plunging to 35,839 ft. (10,923m), the Mariana Trench is the deepest underwater valley.

Ice rivers

Glaciers are huge rivers of ice that flow through mountain valleys. They usually move about 6 ft. (2m) a day.

Watch out!

Avalanches are huge piles of snow that can crash down a mountainside faster than a speeding car. They can be set off by melting snow or even by skiers.

Peak heroine

In 1995 Alison Hargreaves became the first woman to reach the summit of Everest alone and without bottled oxygen. Tragically, she died the same year on the K2 peak.

13

Fantastic Plants

Plants are truly amazing. Not only can they make their own food using air, water, and sunlight, they can also survive in all sorts of places and conditions.

Huge ... and smelly

The stinking corpse lily has the biggest flower in the world. Its monster bloom, which smells like rotting fish, can be up to 3 ft. (90cm) across. But the flower of the Devil's Tongue arum lily smells so awful that it makes people faint!

STINKING CORPSE LILY

DEVIL'S TONGUE

Cultivating miniature bonsai trees has become very popular. These trees originally came from Japan where their name means "to plant in shallow dishes."

To bee or not to bee?

The flower of the bee orchid looks and smells like a bee, so that it can attract real bees to its pollen.

Tiny trees

Unlike rain forest trees, which can be as tall as a 20-story building, Arctic willows are only an inch or two tall. They grow close to the ground to protect themselves from biting winds.

Help!

Towering tree
The most massive tree on earth is a giant sequoia in California called "General Sherman." It stands 275 ft. (83m) tall and contains enough wood to make 5 billion matches.

Goodbye fly!
Did you know that some plants eat insects? Whenever a fly lands on a Venus flytrap, the plant's leaves snap shut, trapping the fly inside. The fly is then dissolved in acids and eaten by the plant.

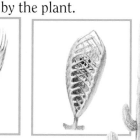

The candlestick cactus
The saguaro is the largest cactus in the world. It grows in the deserts of the U.S. and Mexico and can reach 58 ft. (17m) high. That's about as tall as a five-story building.

Fatal fungus
The death cap fungus is deadly poisonous, even in tiny amounts. It causes 90 percent of all deaths resulting from fungus poisoning.

Wow!

Animal Records

Most people know that all the animals in the world belong to one animal group or another. But do *you* know the main differences between some of these animal groups? Here's your chance to find out!

Quiz

1. Which animals breathe air, look after their young and feed them milk, and have bodies that are covered with hair or fur?

2. Which animals have scaly skins, usually lay eggs, and have bodies that are the same temperature as the air around them?

3. Which animals also have bodies that are covered in scales and breathe through special flaps called gills?

4. Which animals have six legs, a head, and a body that is divided into two parts called the thorax and the abdomen?

1. Mammals
2. Reptiles
3. Fishes
4. Insects

Big bird, little bird

The biggest bird of all, the ostrich, grows up to 9 ft. (2.7m) tall and is so heavy it can't fly. The tiny bee hummingbird is the smallest bird in the world and measures just 2.3 in. (5.7cm). It's an expert at flying, beating its wings 80 times per second so that it can hover on the spot and even fly backward.

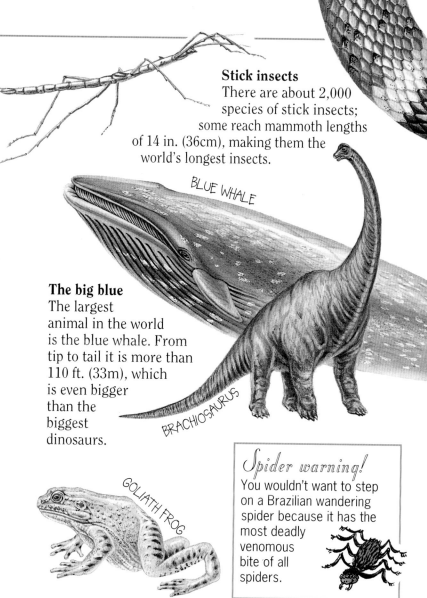

Stick insects
There are about 2,000 species of stick insects; some reach mammoth lengths of 14 in. (36cm), making them the world's longest insects.

BLUE WHALE

The big blue
The largest animal in the world is the blue whale. From tip to tail it is more than 110 ft. (33m), which is even bigger than the biggest dinosaurs.

BRACHIOSAURUS

GOLIATH FROG

Spider warning!
You wouldn't want to step on a Brazilian wandering spider because it has the most deadly venomous bite of all spiders.

Jumbo frog
At 13.6 in. (34cm), the goliath frog from Africa is the giant of all frogs. The females are larger than the males and they can weigh 7.3 lb. (3.3kg).

This coral snake is one of the most poisonous reptiles on earth.

Countries of the World

There are about 195 independent countries in the world. This number changes: countries come and go as a result of wars or diplomatic agreements.

Big country

The biggest country in the world is, without a doubt, Russia. If you traveled by train from Vladivostock, which is in the east of Russia, to Moscow, which is in the west, the journey would take you eight days.

Country stroll

The world's smallest country is the Vatican City in Italy. It is so tiny, it would take you about an hour and a half to walk around its border.

Not another one!

Nursery news

Did you know that the African country Malawi has the highest recorded birth rate in the world? Between 1985 and 1990 about 56 babies were born there for every 1,000 people.

Country crowds

If you don't like crowds, don't go to China! More people live in China than in any other country in the world. In 1995, the number of people living there reached 1.2 billion!

Globe trotters' quiz

Here's your chance to go on a
sightseeing trip around the world.

*1. In which country would
you find this magical marble
tomb called the Taj Mahal?*

*2. If you wanted to take a
snapshot of this colorful
cathedral, would you
have to go to Russia,
Iceland, or Greece?*

*3. If you were going out for a
night at the opera in this
building, where would you be?*

*4. Which country's
capital boasts this
famous tower?*

*5. Where in
the world
can you see
the longest
wall ever
built?*

*6. Where would you come
across these giant stone
heads?*

1. India. 2. Russia. 3. Australia. 4. France. 5. China. 6. U.S.

City Check

In 1800 there were about 954 million people in the world. By the year 2000, experts reckon that there will be more than 6 billion people on earth. What's more, over half of them will be living in cities and towns.

Top cities

100 years ago:	Year 2000:
London	Tokyo–Yokohama
4,231,431	29,971,000
Paris	Mexico City
2,423,946	27,872,000
Peking (Beijing)	São Paulo
1,648,814	25,354,000
Canton (Kwangchow)	Seoul
1,600,000	21,976,000
Berlin	Bombay
1,579,244	15,357,000

Pooh!
The world's largest landfill is on Staten Island, New York. It covers 2,965 acres (1,186 hectares) and contains 100,000 tons of garbage.

Going up

Land in cities is very expensive, so modern buildings are often tall and thin to take up less space. The first skyscraper was completed in Chicago in 1885. It was 10 stories high.

Canary Wharf
London
805 ft.
(244m)

Sears Tower
Chicago
1,454 ft.
(436m)

Nina Tower
Hong Kong
(year 2000)
1,792 ft. (543m)

City squeeze

Many of the people who work in Japan's cities can't afford to live in the city centers, so they take a train to work. These trains are so overcrowded that guards have to push people onto them.

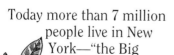

Firefree city

La Paz in Bolivia is nearly a fireproof city. This is 12,000 ft. (3,600m) above sea level. At that height, the air is so thin that it has hardly enough oxygen to keep a fire blazing.

From New Amsterdam ... to New York

New York was founded by Dutch settlers in 1626. At that time it was called New Amsterdam and was little more than a fort, a windmill, and 30 houses ...

During the 1600s thousands of settlers arrived, mainly from Europe. In 1811 a grid pattern of streets was built for the growing city. And by 1871, the city's population had reached 1 million.

Today more than 7 million people live in New York—"the Big Apple." It is one of the most crowded and exciting cities on earth.

Superstructures

Thousands of years ago, a Greek writer made a list of the seven most awesome man-made structures of his day. (Sadly, all of these structures—except for the

Pyramids—have now collapsed.) He would have been pretty impressed by today's eye-popping structures!

Super Seto
At 8.2 miles (13km) long, the Seto–Ohasi Bridge in Japan is the longest combined road and rail bridge in the world.

Tall tale
The Empire State Building in New York is 102 stories high, and one of the tallest buildings in the world. It is also one of the luckiest. In 1945 a B25 bomber plane crashed into the 79th floor at 250 mph (400kmh) ... and the building remained standing.

Hotel from Atlantis
The world's only underwater hotel is in Florida. Controlled air pressure inside the hotel stops it from flooding, and guests have to scuba dive to their rooms!

Huge home

The palace of the Sultan of Brunei is the largest lived-in palace in the world. It has 1,788 rooms, 257 bathrooms, and enough garage space for the Sultan's 110 cars. If you went on a tour of the house and spent just half a minute in each room, it would take you over a day!

Journey under the sea

The longest undersea tunnel in the world is the Channel Tunnel, linking Britain to France. It was started in 1987 and completed in 1994 at a bank-breaking $15 billion. Using the Chunnel, it takes just 21 minutes to cross the Channel; by ferry it would take an hour and a half.

Big Buddha

There are plenty of tall statues in the world, but the tallest one of all is a 396 ft. (120m) high bronze statue of the holy man Buddha. This statue, which was completed in Tokyo, Japan, in 1993 is so huge that three young children can sit on one of its toe nails, with room to spare!

Staying in Touch

People have kept in touch by letter for centuries. Today we can use more instant means of communication such as phones, faxes, or computers.

The first postage stamp was used in 1840. This early stamp fetched a record-breaking price of $3.7 million at auction.

Inventive!

Ancient Sumerians carried messages on stone tablets.

Aborigines used drums to "talk" to people far away.

Native American people sent smoke signals into the air.

Cable call

When you talk on the phone, your voice is turned into flashes of light that travel along hair-thin glass strands called optical fibers. One pair of optical fibers can carry 8,000 telephone conversations, all going on at once.

FIBER OPTIC CABLE

Satellites

Communications satellites in space receive television, telephone, fax, and computer signals from one country and beam them down to another. The world's most powerful satellite can handle 120,000 telephone calls and three color TV channels at any one time.

Fax facts

When you feed a letter into a fax machine, your letter's message is turned into electrical signals. These signals then whiz along telephone cables to another fax machine, which prints out a copy of your letter.

MAGNIFIED FAX IMAGE

Picture this

The days of talking on the phone in scruffy clothes are nearly over! Companies have started making phones with TV-like screens. This means that two speakers can see each other on the screen while on the phone.

R.S.V.P.

This plaque is fixed to the *Pioneer 10* space probe, which left our solar system in 1983 and is heading ever deeper into space. It gives directions for how to find Earth and shows what humans look like. Perhaps one day it will be found by another intelligent species.

POSTCARD TO OUTER SPACE

Surfing the net

The Internet is a network that links computers around the world. It enables people with Internet-linked computers to swap information with each other quickly and easily.

Talking All Over the World

Did you know that 3,000 different languages are spoken all over the world? Some of them are spoken by millions of people. Others are understood by just a handful of remaining native speakers and may soon die out altogether.

Which languages are these?

1. Cocorico
2. Cock-a-doodle-doo
3. Cucurica
4. Chicchirichi

1. French, 2. English
3. Romanian, 4. Italian

SUMERIAN TABLET

Picture writing
The ancient Sumerians were the first people to write down their language, in about 3500 B.C. The writing on this tablet is a promise from the king of Ur to the goddess Innin.

Leading languages
These top three languages have the following number of native speakers:
Chinese (Mandarin) 901 million
English 350 million
Hindi 327 million

Whistled words
Men belonging to the Mazateco tribe in Mexico are such good whistlers that they can hold whole conversations just by whistling!

1. नमस्ते

2. γεια σας

3. привéт

4. もしもし

5. 你 好

Hello!
Can you guess where these different ways of writing "hello" come from?

1. India
2. Greece
3. Russia
4. Japan
5. China

Reading Braille
Blind people use their fingertips to read. Their alphabet is called Braille and is made up of raised dots on paper.

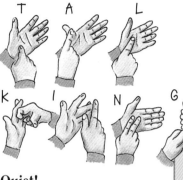

Talking in silence
Not all languages are spoken. Deaf people and others who cannot use a spoken language often "chat" using hand signals.

Quiet!
In Warramunga, Australia women are not allowed to speak for up to a year after their husbands die. During this time they talk using hand and arm signals. Some women get so used to this way of chatting that they use it even when they are allowed to speak again.

What a mouthful!
The full name for Krung Thep Bangkok, the capital of Thailand, is 175 letters long. Luckily, there is an official short version ... it's only got 111 letters (and no capitals—they are not used in Thai).

Language lowdown

- Papua New Guinea in the Pacific Ocean is not a very big place. Yet about 869 separate languages are spoken there.

- The world's longest alphabet, which is used in Cambodia, has 74 letters.

- The world's shortest alphabet, which is used in the Solomon Islands, has only 11 letters.

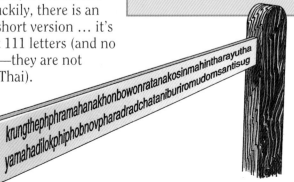

krungthephphramahanakhonbowonratanakosinmahintharayutha
yamahadilokphiphobnovpharadradchataniburiromudomsantisug

27

On the Move

For thousands of years, traveling was a very slow business. People had to rely on animals, animal-drawn vehicles, and boats powered by sails or oars get from place to place. Today, the all-time speed record is 24,791 mph (39,666kmh), set by the *Apollo 10* spacecraft in 1969.

That's fast

A daredevil named Andy Green will try to break the land-speed record by reaching 800 mph (1,280kmh). His car, called Thrust SSC, has about the same power as 140 racing cars.

THRUST SSC

Car comforts

The most outrageous car must be the 50-seat Cadillac called "Hollywood Dream." It comes fitted with bathtub, bedroom, swimming pool, theater, and even a miniature golf course!

Wash and go

In 1994 Graeme Obree of Great Britain set the world's one-hour track cycling record on ... a homemade bike. He built it from all sorts of bits and pieces, including part of a washing machine.

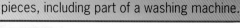

Underwater giant

Russian typhoon submarines weigh in at a colossal 26,500 tons. Six of these super-subs are thought to be lurking under the ocean waves.

Railroad rocket

A French train called the TGV is the world's fastest train on rails! It whizzes between the cities of Paris and Lyon at an average speed of 132 mph (212.5kmh). That's more than twice as fast as a car on a freeway.

How big?

The biggest ship anywhere in the world is a huge oil tanker called *Jahre Viking*. Four football fields could be laid end to end on its deck—and there would still be room to spare.

Express service

The Lockheed SR-71 Blackbird is the fastest jet aircraft in the skies. In 1974 it flew across the Atlantic Ocean, from New York to London, in just under two hours.

Flying incognito

This Lockheed F117A fighter plane is nicknamed the Stealth fighter because it is impossible to detect on the radar screens of its enemies. Why? It is made of materials that soak up radar signals instead of reflecting them.

Motorcycle madness

Believe it or not, a man in Australia named Harry was so fond of his motorcycle that he married it! The motorcycle's name was Mildred.

Eco-facts

Pollution is not just about dirty air and filthy water. Sadly, we can spoil our environment in many other ways, and these are all kinds of pollution.

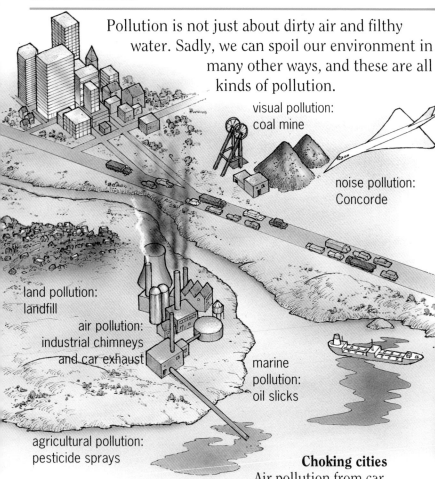

visual pollution: coal mine

noise pollution: Concorde

land pollution: landfill

air pollution: industrial chimneys and car exhaust

marine pollution: oil slicks

agricultural pollution: pesticide sprays

Garbage!

The countries producing the most garbage per head per year are …

U.S.
1,861 lb.
(846kg)

Canada
1,375 lb.
(625kg)

Finland
1,109 lb.
(504kg)

Choking cities

Air pollution from car, factory, and power-plant fumes is often at its worst in summer, because the fumes react with sunlight to create smog. Los Angeles is one of the most smog-bound cities in the world.

Rotten rain

Poisonous gases from factories and power plants rise into the air and mix with water vapor to make acid rain. Rain that fell on Pitlochry, Scotland, on April 10, 1974, was as acidic as lemon juice!

Stunted growth

Tree rings show how much a tree grows each year. Cross sections of trees damaged by acid rain reveal how growth has been slowed down.

Crumbling statues

Acid rain is eating away at the stonework of many of the world's historic city landmarks.

Ozone holes

Ozone in the atmosphere protects us from the Sun's harmful rays. Chemicals that we use can destroy this ozone. Scientists have found ozone holes over both the North Pole and the South Pole.

Look out!

Pollution is nothing new. Before drains and sewers had been invented, people often threw their garbage and dirty water right out onto the street.

Save our trees!

Did you know that 75,000 trees could be spared each week by recycling the Sunday edition of the *New York Times*?

Recycled cans

Half the aluminum drink cans in the U.S. are melted down, remade, refilled, and back on supermarket shelves within six weeks of being thrown away.

INDEX

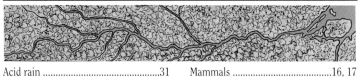

Published in 1997 by Creative Education
123 South Broad Street
Mankato, Minnesota 56001
Creative Education is an imprint of
The Creative Company
Cover design by Eric Madsen
Illustrations by Julian Baker, Charlotte Hard
and Bill Donohoe
Photographs by Austin J. Brown; British
Telecommunications; Frank Spooner/Gamma;
Hutchison Library; NHPA/Kevin Schafer, B&C
Alexander, David Middleton; Oxford Scientific
Films/Harold Taylor, E.R. Degginger, Andrew Park,
Survival Anglia, Matthias, Hackenberg,
Imamura, First
Text © HarperCollins Publishers Ltd. 1996
Illustrations © HarperCollins Publishers Ltd. 1996
Published by arrangement with
HarperCollins Publishers.

**Library of Congress
Cataloging-in-Publication Data**
Around the world.
p. cm. - (It's a fact!)
Includes index.
ISBN 0-88682-863-5

1. Curiosities and wonders-Juvenile literature.
I. Creative Education, Inc. (Mankato, Minn.)
II. Series.
AG243.W595 1997   96-41217
031.02-dc20
EDCBA